I0232459

Of Dust and Dreams

A Collection of Poetry and Quotes

A mosaic of longing, loss, and the quiet
beauty of being

Uzan Swu & Rukuthonu Vitsu

Second Edition

ink Scribe

Of Dust and Dreams

Publisher: Inkscribe Publishing. Pvt. Ltd.

ISBN: 978-1-969259-04-3

CONTENTS

Oh! When you receive the right love from the wrong
person amidst chaotic world.

-Uzan Swu

Of Dust and Dreams 5

MONSIEUR IN GREY

While I sloped by the rack to paint your face,
I saw you striking and cold in grey suit
With dim gleaming eyes burdened with vast wave.
Oh! Made my heart sink deep and eyes run brut

Your face rests flawless; proceeds my portrait
Perfect gentleman you are by mild guts
With such fine virtue, turns me a poet
My soul rumbled down; portrait turned to fuss

Loving you comes through great grief with restraint
Thus, with patience, ought to bring you to being
Oh at-last oh! How splendid is the paint.
Your portrait seems beyond pleased and soothing

By the fall of night, in time took my rest
And by my work in time dealt with, felt blest.

-Uzan Swu

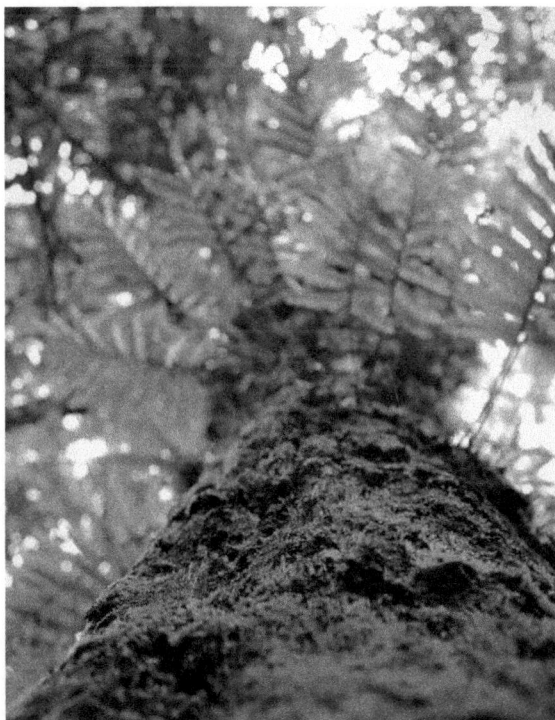

When the freezing misty wind embarrasses the tiny
dewy leaves making them dance in the broad
horizon of the hazy blue sky, my soul wholly rejoices
in bliss of such view.

-Uzan Swu

THE WEIGHT OF FEELING

I am the grief in a mother's sigh,
The echo of a lover's last goodbye.
I am the silence of a room too wide,
The weight of words that none confide.

I am the ring on trembling hands,
The promise made, the shifting sands.
I am the hope that waits in vain,
The shadow cast by unseen pain.

I am the tear, the laugh, the ache,
The hollow void, the heart that breaks.
In a world that feels in endless streams,
Am I real, or just their dreams?

-Rukuthonu Vitsu

The silence of the earth is troubled when a tiny shiny droplet makes its journey through the clouds and taps the drowsy leaves on the trees launching the wondrous soothing war of earth.

-Uzan Swu

The vivid giant mountains grew softly hazy as the glittering rain marched down unnumbered in rage.

-Uzan Swu

A CRUSH REVERIE

In your proximity, my heart hastens,
A smile blooms effortlessly upon my face.
Each glimpse of you, a joy profound,
Brightening my world with boundless love.

Daily, I yearn for your gentle gaze,
To dispel shadows with your radiant glow.
Though fate keeps us worlds apart,
You're the melody that soothes my heart.

Secretly, I harbour an immense infatuation,
You, the architect of dreams unplanned.
Unaware, yet a source of my delight,
In your presence, worries dissolve into ether.

So here I am, with words untold,
A heart aflame, a love to unfurl.
Though we may never walk as two,
Know you're cherished, through and through.

-Rukuthonu Vitsu

The tranquilizing sound of the rain we take pleasure
in meditating can also be a melancholic cry of
sorrow from the misty clouds.

-Uzan Swu

A World of Feelings

Someone laughs as vows are spoken,
Someone weeps with heart left broken.
Someone waits though hope has faded,
Someone sits alone, unaided.

Someone sings with joy so bright,
Someone drowns in endless night.
Someone finds, someone has lost,
Love blooms, love turns to frost.

In this world of joy and sorrow,
Where do I belong tomorrow?
If I feel it all inside,
Am I the sea or just the tide?

-Rukuthonu Vitsu

Took me eternal to untangle my dismayed heart just
to realize it was actually all empty.

-Uzan Swu

UNADDRESSED

The dawn brought sixteen pilgrims forth the road
That marked the sail to peace and harmony
Marching forth boldly, stamping the bare road
As they progressed, caroled in assembly

Sang "we rose to find it", "ought to find it!"
God knows if they were howling or chanting,
Their tune roared so sharp made the plum leaves slit
Trip ceased as they caught one clan advancing.

In trice there were shouts and screams far and wide
That closed in stumbling, pounding and bleeding
After the clash, blinding dust stormed the wind
Dust filled of desires, greed and still doubting

Fools they were for abandoning their quest
Peace and harmony thus left unaddressed.

-Uzan Swu

A hole lays in the depth of my heart which is far
from the reach of my soul but is felt in the dept of
my dreams."

-Uzan Swu

WHAT ESCAPE FEELS LIKE

Wary and bounded by the darkness, I kept searching for an escape.

Sadly, I had not known of what escape felt like, until...

Until I felt a puny rain drop slide down my warm rosy cheeks.

Until I felt the dusky golden leaves carefully land on my shoulders.

Until I felt the chilly mossy green grass growing by the trees.

Until I felt the soft unpolluted breeze stroke my cheeks.

leaving behind its warm mellow kiss.

Until I felt the busy crystal river jump into my hands as I swiftly dipped it inside.

Until I witnessed the beauty of the glittering lights, far away in distant hills

by the frosty dark night.

Until my eyes landed on the tiny crawling glowworms that twinkled

like starts as the sun takes its leave to rest.

Until I witnessed the hazel leaves slow dancing by the momentum of the wind.

through the tiny wooden window of my kitchen.

Certainly, I had not known what escape felt like until I experienced the

rustic life I did not know I needed.

-Uzan Swu

The reason my tangled past exist is to sway me off my warm feet and keep me brawling through the storm to never give in.

-Uzan Swu

SCENT

Your fragrance is as captivating as the roses,
As vibrant as the tulips,
As delightful as freshly baked cakes,
As refreshing as ripe fruits,
and as tempting as the finest delicacies.

You possess a unique and unparalleled scent
One that perfectly aligns with my heart.
It's a fragrance I can always recognize,
one that irresistibly draws me towards you.

-Rukuthonu Vitsu

With gentle easiness the rain slowly slides down the
tin roof in soft whispers as I crawl under my blanket
and melt by the sound.

-Uzan Swu

EVERLASTING SOUL

This tiny warm heart shatters and mourns in utmost
woe.
As I lay somewhere far away failing to bid you
farewell.
Sleep denies on me as the memories flashes before
my vision,
The world failed to discover the beauty that was
within you.

Or was it you who never allowed that garden bloom
enough for
the word to see.
How beautiful it would have been, you were the
kindest and
 warmest soul ever!
Oh! Yet it is always the most beautiful flower that
are picked
 first from the garden.

Thus, I instead mourn for the world to have lost a
soul as you.

Through this song I lay my vow, time shall pass by
and by

But this heart shall never forget your goodness to
the end.

-Uzan Swu

(To a soul who deserved the world)

I felt the taste of bitter syrup at the tip of my tongue as the grey clouds emerged however it was washed down by the taste of a tinder honey syrup as the tiny rain droplets danced its way down the earth.

-Uzan Swu

MARIANS, NOT PRISON

Miles from home hills of remote where I dwell
Amidst proud titan hills rests my stay
A house loaded with boundless laws and love
Which some day tastes bitter but mostly sugary

Assumed by people as an obliged vicious prison
Unaware that prison solely holds faulty vile crowds
Thus liberty overflows for people with no offense
Foremost dispute follows lame and fallacious
mindset

House was led by a surely kind but partly stern sister
Whose existence alone flows like a soothing breeze
Nourished and guided us with endless values of life
Through time I gained mighty peace and wisdom

Warm and cozy gently it grew as my heart laid
comfortable,
In a circle packed with diverse vivid personalities.
All tailored together to battle through the quick
whimsical journey.

-Uzan Swu

When the sky gets darker and cold, I shut my eyes
and feel your warm soul lingering by my side.

-Uzan Swu

You Are My East

You are my East, where the sun does rise,
A beacon of light in morning skies.
With you begins my every day,
In your glow, I find my way.

You are my East, where rivers start,
Flowing gently to my heart.
Your words, a soothing, gentle stream,
In your voice, I find my theme.

You are my East, where mountains stand,
Strong and steady, hand in hand.
In your strength, I find my peace,
With you, my worries find release.

-Rukuthonu Vitsu

In the depth of trembling darkness my soul cries for you yet my heart sweeps you away by the arrival of daylight.

-Uzan Swu

DISGUISED LOVE

Some folk curse love, yet some honor it.

What is love? It emerges and bear away something
or the other.

Why does it feel so reliable yet unreliable?

It emerges and runs off within a delightful yet tragic
closing.

Why is it utmost delightful yet most dreadful?

For disguised it comes, allegiance one makes in love
alters everything.

Wise man glorifies and fools mourns, fragile trips
and strong survives

But, alas, folk no longer reside for love but for lust.

Will true love get by past with time? a question to
dwell upon.

William Shakespeare once had a dear dark lady in his
life, so do us.

Will thy dark lady save thee or drown thee?

We shall start to seek true love, so that it begins to
seek us, and to spare us.

-Uzan Swu

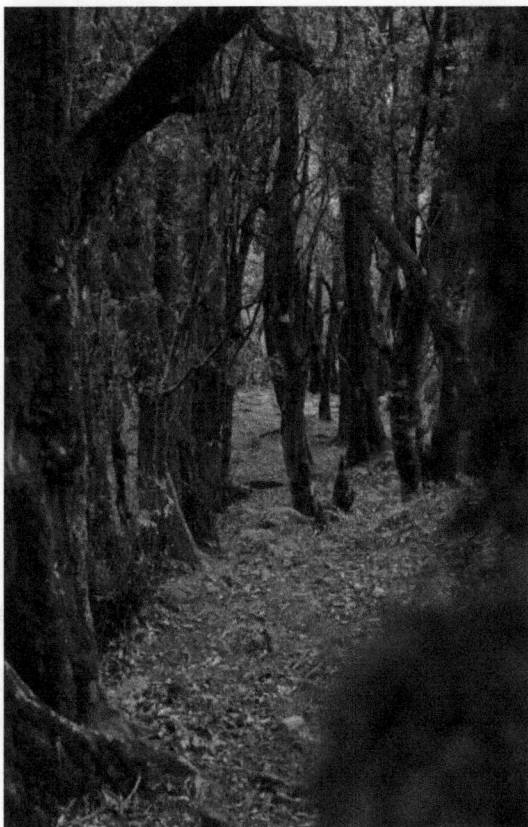

Sliding my hands under your mellow hands, I gently followed you as we disappeared deep into my dreams.

-Uzan Swu

AS WE DEPART

Is there a sense of nostalgia on the bus?
Is there a face that it prefers?
Do its worn seats mutter about moments
They'll never forget as we depart?

As we look out the windows,
following the raindrops as they race,
Does the bus wish it could embrace
us with its steel arms?

Does it subtly convey our laughter,
as if it were a secret it wishes to share?
When we part ways at the end of the ride,
does it miss our silent exhalations?

I pondered and asked,
"Does the bus contain dreams like ours,
Of journeys that last forever,
and passengers it never outgrew?"

-Rukuthonu Vitsu

I adored you by the day and dreamt you by the night.

-Uzan Swu

TO MY BLISS

A weary sphere was the world to dwell by,
Loaded with lurking hoaxes and serpents.
Amidst the turmoil, there's no place for me.
Left to wander lone within packed merchants.

Yet soon life had best present to offer,
An enchanting soft soul I was blessed with.
A girl tangled in kindness to offer.
The mellow breeze rejoiced as we spoke more.

In utmost swift our quiet chain kept growing
Thus, the dry weary sphere soon turned blissful
The blunt path advanced with our goals merging
After which through thick and thin cheerful

My soul thus blooms in grace in thy presence
This heart will ever embrace thy essence

-Uzan Swu

Pdf or Word doc they inquired.... "a cup of coffee!"
I exclaimed.

-Uzan Swu

A SILENT PAGE

In the book of life, so full and wide,
A silent page, untouched, left behind.
No ink to stain its virgin face,
A quiet space in a crowded place.

Around it's stories of love and sorrow,
Of victories bright and shadows low.
Each word a scratch, each line a wound,
A path traced from near to far around.

But this single page, so pure, so quiet,
Awaits the pen, the writer's choice.
No hasty hand, no wild scrawl,
Just room to breathe, to catch it all.

In its silence, dreams might grow,
A fertile field for thoughts to sow.
It carries the promise yet unseen,
Of what could be, of might have been.

Not void, but with potential rife,
A canvas for the dance of life.
It's quiet speaks, a subtle call,
To those who listen, hear it all.

So don't be afraid of the silent page,
For in its calm, all stories blend.
A soft beginning, a quiet push,
A space where potential plods.

For all stories ever being told,
A silent beginning, pure and true.
A page of silence, a waiting start,
The cradle of a beating heart.

-Rukuthonu Vitsu

I do not love you, yet your absence fills my chest, an
ache without a name, a yearning I can't understand.

-Rukuthonu Vitsu

I pour my soul my every breath into the fire that
love begets yet you weigh my scars against your own,
blind to the life I've overthrown.

-Rukuthonu Vitsu

FAIR GENTLEMAN

My fine fair Gentleman of frozen heart
What keeps thee thus pale and lifeless
My puny heart splits apart by that part
With such glimpse of thee I am left reckless

My cold fair prince in prime mystical suit
What are thee made of that burns me to dust?
And yet my bold charm of flames keeps you mute
Oh! What keeps you away from my fierce gust?

Perhaps my spell of flames was ne'er mighty
Or rather thy spell was overly firm
Thus, leaving me quite futile and empty,
Beneath ocean filled with crumbled charm.

Yet, these bold feelings ought to stand timeless
And dwell like a nightingale's song endless

-Uzan Swu

His love for her was a masterpiece painted with sincerity, but her words were mere brushstrokes of deception, creating a portrait of heartbreak.

-Rukuthonu Vitsu

HAZY VISION

With time slipping by, my sight grew hazy
Without glasses, tangled in unclear realm
Bleaklessly lost amidst blurry city
Yet by my glasses often leaded calm

With each blazing fleeting day, I ponder
Burdened by the vision that goes murky.
Failing fairly to recall folks harder,
Filled with harsh misery lost in journey.

Oft cheered up grasping it as a blessing,
As I no longer could lay sight on men.
Seems like a gesture pure from Lord testing,
Yet swiftly caught used to live by no men.

In time acquired to dwell by this sight,
At times oddly young to be in this fight.

-Uzan Swu

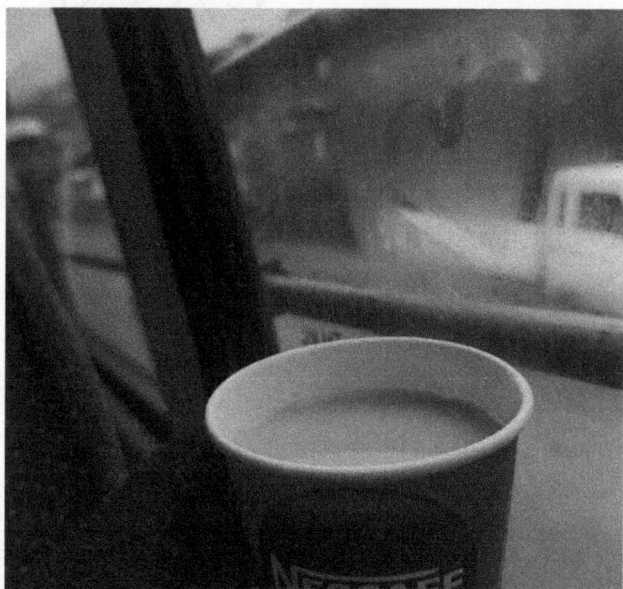

The coffee you buy for me tastes sweeter, as if infused with love itself. Its aroma, a scent of affection, fills my senses with warmth and comfort.

-Rukuthonu Vitsu

DEMENTIA LOVE

You were eternally my favorite book,
Thus, chapters after chapters we composed.
I grasped and loved every bit of that look,
Oh! Since this vile plague leaves every route closed.

You were gracefully my favorite book
Yet kept dropping the page I was into.
And kept losing trail of all our daybook.
All cherished chapters were now in two.

As clock travelled by, his warm face blurred dry
Thus, gently lost the scent that I dwelled by.
Solely thing obvious was faintly his eye,
Which oftentimes filled with tears, don't know why.

I soon flew far from the reach of my soul,
And far astray from the reach of your call.

-Uzan Swu

In the quiet of dawn, as coffee's warmth caressed,
pondered I: what if we let others be, and in our own
paths, peacefully invest?

-Rukuthonu Vitsu

UNSIGHTED LAND

Oh sightless land of mine, all of glorious warriors
Warriors that formerly ushered the land valiantly
What withholds thee visionless and oblivious to
actuality?
Bids adieu the past, thus imparting the future to
thee.

Truly like a flimsy mislaid fly are thee,
Trampled by the paws of dominant folks deftly.
What makes thee thus visionless amidst late ages?
Certainly, the wicked urge of power and wealth.

Each sole day, a weary mother mislays a cherished
child
Astute, bright and fitted virtuous child slinging
oneself!
Utterly due to grievous prejudiced care beneath the
dominant
The utmost renowned regime chiefs assumed to
steer thee

Oh awful weary land of mine, thriving in muted
tongue

How many unstained little ones do thee inclined to
lose?

The cry that is coffined today, slays countless
tomorrow.

Thus let this song be thy lead to soar aloft and brawl

To unfold the shivered voices for the imminent
generation

And pave an upright route for the infinite
undeserved

-Uzan Swu

The moon and stars retreat behind the clouds
tonight, their veiled presence suggesting an intimate
awareness of the unspoken currents flowing between
us.

-Rukuthonu Vitsu

PARADISE IN NAGALAND

Dwelling in unknown City miles away,
City full of smuts and cries far and wide.
Over time I grew homesick day-to-day
In dew twilight, adored pine trees in wild.

I rest by the window as the daybreak.
The crisp fresh sight mimicked Dzukou valley,
Where the Tragopan stirred round by the lake.
Sweet folk songs from fields echoed the valley.

Soon, noontide turned icy, dim and misty,
Sight that recalls me of mighty Mithun.
Walked through the mist, relished the true beauty,
A dew drop taps my palm thus gains vision.

Learns that while seeking bliss of false surprise
Missed that Nagas now own a paradise.

-Uzan swu

At day's end, we're but melancholy souls, seeking light in realms where switches lay dormant.

-Rukuthonu Vitsu

RUBY RED TEEN

My voyage began with me being sixteen,
Thus, in midst of crowd, hunched by the window
In Ruby Red shirt, saw a handsome teen,
Hence seized my utmost gaze and stole my flow.

The clock slowly ceased in your presence,
A rush ne'er sensed before rushed right through me.
All things became vibrant past your entrance.
By time kept liking you until you flee.

Ages passed yet this rush ne'er ceased for once.
Oh! It's been tiring years of yearning,
Since felt the mild gust as you closer comes.
Now solely flashbacks are faintly burning.

By every advance, you strayed miles away
Left me wholly ragged feeling astray.

-Uzan Swu

I loved you silently, from the shadows where you couldn't see, my gaze seeks you, knowing we're destined to remain apart. I cast my wishes on a fleeting stars and smile at the moon, carrying a love that only the night understands.

-Rukuthonu Vitsu

Let's meet tonight, beneath the moon's soft silver light, betwixt the blossoms' fragrant sigh, Beneath the rendition of a starlit sky. I'll wait for you with bated breath, as the shadows mingle, and dream beget.

-Rukuthonu Vitsu

SHE IS US

Dwelling in the world of grand disarray
Oh angel! Living by fair way, are you?
No truth comes in peace for us to obey
Thus, to stomp o'er wicked desires, can you?

Weak as a blossom is she, without Christ
Yet, being wise as Deborah the prophet,
All yearnings and thirsts ought to remain fright
And she shall bloom and dwell as a poppet.

Untrue and faithless is she, without Christ
Yet, being true as Ruth the amenable,
All evil and fraud ought to remain fright
And she shall grow ever unshakeable.

She in fair time attained her utmost worth
And ne'er looking back again marched straight forth.

-Uzan Swu
(Tribute to VVSBA Women)

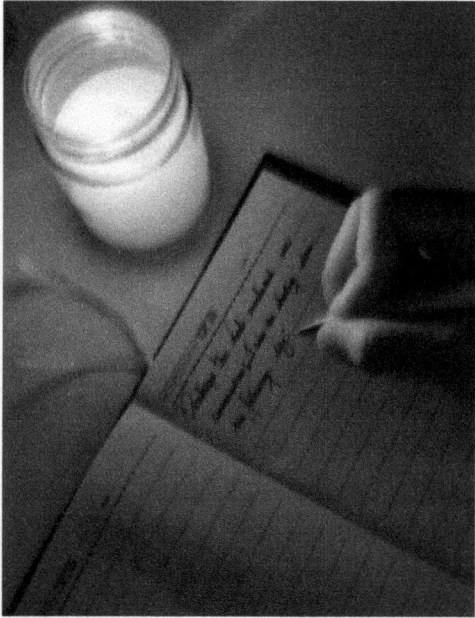

In the quite intimacy of ink on paper, I pour out my heart in letters never meant to be read. Each word a confession, each sentence a longing, penned for the eyes of my lover yet destined to remain a secret treasure of my soul.

-Rukuthonu Vitsu

Tussle Of Me

Strolling in dark endless woods, I pondered
Then out of the clouded silence emerged Hate,
Addressed me as her, as she moved closer.
Artificial puppet is what she labeled us.

Realized shortly, the actual truth within me is Her.
Yet we were both indeed an awful paradox.
Though one we are, she was a loner and I the lover.
In every way she failed, failed miserably to win me
over.

I'm not hate, I fought for peace in the deepest dept
of misery,
I gently embraced her to be merged as one, I won
through her.
Willing she wholly gave in, glad to be accepted
Breaking all ties around us burst in tears as i
embraced her.

Love is key to succeed over all hatred of the world,
Within a flash the bleak remorse in me faded.
Hate is my sorrowful past and love my mellow
present
Weak is my cruel past and strongest my prideful
present.

-Uzan Swu

No stars can speak it, no galaxies contain,
No moon reflects it, no words can explain.
Once, the universe was my solace, my all,
But now, it is you who answers my call.
Deeper than eternity, stronger than fate,
My love for you is the infinite state.

-Rukuthonu Vitsu

It's past midnight, and the silence screams your name. I don't know what to do but write, spilling feelings I should have spoken aloud. How lost am I to miss you this much?

-Rukuthonu Vitsu

I ache for the dead so much that I wish time would
abandon me, letting me join them. But if it did,
would I then mourn the living, left behind in a world
I can no longer touch?

-Rukuthonu Vitsu

SISTER OF BLISS

Chaos and longing mankind this world was loaded
with,
When an angelic gift from heavens above was sent
A sister, blessed and amiable who is more than a
sister
Filled truly with wonders tangled in infinite love.

Through thick and thin lingered around steering my
way
As a shepherd redeems his sheep from passing astray
Sheltered me against giant odds, resting taller than a
lighthouse
The wicked thus feared your utmost presence upon
me

Was formerly dull and fragile till you gracefully
molded me
Unwisely deserted harsh corrections once, to be free
Yet boundless love of yours always lingered by
Thus withstood the cruel world to be the soul I am
this day

If heavens please allow me to dwell as your sister
once more

Uncounted deeds of yours will be forgotten
nevermore

Thus will remain to abide in this wondrous song
forevermore

-Uzan Swu

(To my precious sister)

What are you? The solace and serenity you wove into my life, I didn't grasp their worth until they slipped away. You offered me something beyond measure, something no one else could ever bestow. And when you departed, you took it all, leaving me hollow and restless. I've sought it in others, but all I've found is a deeper void within. No one else could ever understand or feel the way you did. Tell me, what was this rare and irreplaceable gift you granted, and why does its absence echo so profoundly within me?"

-Rukuthonu Vitsu

In the quiet of our unspoken words, I wonder if
your heart holds a spark like mine, for my soul is
restless in the silence, longing to know if you feel
the same hidden flame.

-Rukuthonu Vitsu

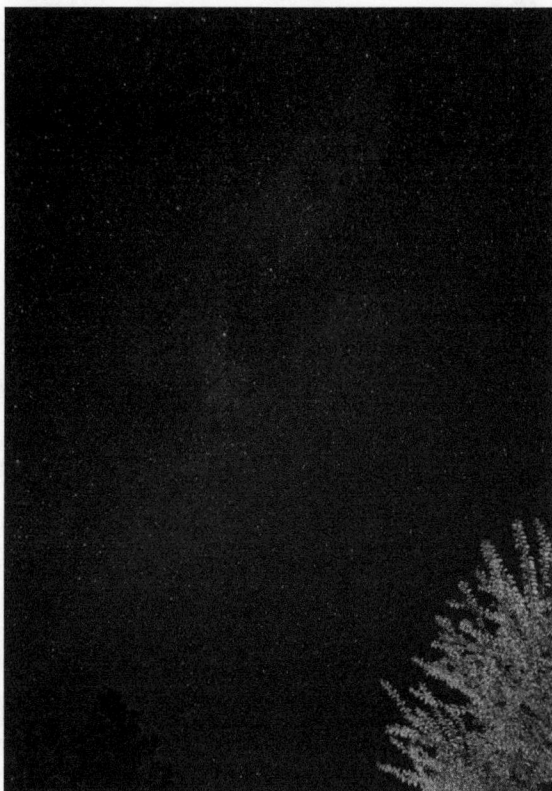

Beneath the vast night sky, I lie on the grass,
scanning the constellations for your sign, longing for
a moment where we could discuss the wonders of
astronomy together.

-Rukuthonu Vitsu

I nurtured a seed with hopes it would bloom for you, but you left before the first petal could unfold, leaving me with the ghost of what might have been.

-Rukuthonu Vitsu

DREAMS

In the stillness of my slumber, you appeared,
we journeyed together, side by side,
through valleys green and valleys steep,
where shadows danced and whispered fears.

Together we faced the trials,
with courage drawn from unseen bonds,
Climbing mountains, crossing streams,
Your voice a guiding star in the night.

In a valley of lilies,
we lay beneath an infinite sky,
watching galaxies spin their tales,
As I spoke of stars and distant worlds.

Nebulas bloomed in the darkness,
like flowers of the cosmos,
And you, a presence warm and kind,
offered truths I longed to hear.

In that dream, we were infinite,
our spirits unencumbered, our hearts unbound,
A world apart, yet deeply connected,
A place I never wanted to leave.

Morning arrived, and you faded,
A shadow slipping from my grasp,
But the dream remains, a gentle whisper,
a reminder of what might be.

In this life, we remain apart,
But in dreams, we are one,
walking valleys, climbing mountains,
forever seeking the stars.

-Rukuthonu Vitsu

In the garden of our existence, our steps diverge in rhythm and pace, yet it is in this contrast that we find a symphony, a melody that celebrates the beauty of being different.

-Rukuthonu Vitsu

FROM HEART IT COMES

We wandered through the valley of moral and evil
Where, witnessed the agony of youth and the aged folks.
We than boosted our flag and charged in aid
None gave in by fear but advanced, as from heart it comes.

Our hearts led the way as we forged ahead
It knows every turn as it comes from the soul of world.
We sealed our eyes and dragged our legs to deliver help
None abide an inch by distrust but advanced, as from heart it comes

Only salient thing wanted in return is the blessings and love of folks
As the most delightful things in life can best be felt by heart.

-Uzan Swu
Tribute to YRCC members (SJU)

Let it be June, let it be July, let it be August; let the seasons change, let the years slip by. What is yours will find its way, and what will be, will be. For He has written a story just for you—trust in Him, and place your hopes fully in His hands.

-Rukuthonu Vitsu

MONOCHROME GIRL

In the midst of the horde, she stands apart,
A monochrome girl with a yearning soul.
Crowded places suffocate, a heavy weight,
Desiring solitude, to elude the hustle and bustle.

Amidst the mayhem, she dreams of boundless
horizons,
Where the symphony of nature calms, and serenity
lies.
With melodies in her ears and a pen poised in her
grasp,
She finds solace in quietude, in the countryside.

Somewhere far away from the hubbub, the throng,
She takes refuge in nature, peaceful and regal.
Beneath the foliage, she encounters serenity,
Unleashing beauty through her lens, with grace.

Surrounded by the forest's quietness, she finds relief,
A monochrome girl, attaining inner calmness.
In the calm interludes, separate from the swarm,
She feels alive, where she truly belongs.

-Rukuthonu Vitsu

In the wake of your departure to the afterlife, the essence of happiness has faded from my grasp, leaving a profound emptiness where joy once resided.

-Rukuthonu Vitsu

DROWSED TO UNITE

Dreams are solely a world of fantasy,
A world full of unpredictable episodes.
I wandered in where lives my real reverie.
To seize a mellow glance and ease my load.

In stillness of warm dark night, I met you
Slipped in slowly where the beaming stars live,
A touch of your mellow glance evermore set me
free.
Yet roused sudden by the chirping birds, left me
partly alive.

In stillness of warm dark night, I met you again.
Humming by the moon till dawn every ache
forgotten,
Ne'er enough of it, we wandered wholly free.
Yet roused by the tick of clock, back to world so
common.

In stillness of dark endless night, I kept dreaming.
Dreaming of you with unreal flawless episodes
Left me surfing deeper in quest of my healing

-Uzan Swu

Embracing the end holds no fear for me; it feels like
a gentle, serene release, a tender embrace that
promises peace.

-Rukuthonu Vitsu

I yearn to love anyone but you, yet the mystery of
who you are eludes me.

-Rukuthonu Vitsu

Tangled Grief Amidst the Shadows

In bleak depth the grief in me kept crawling
Flowing o'er my gentle body wholly
Could take it no more the anguish roaring
Sought to perceive the bug which seemed deadly

My soul further not owns the emotion
Bowing before the woe as its master
In time the warm heart grows wholly frozen
Failing to endure the still world after

Miles and broad roars my wistful emotions
The passion that pierces over the storm
Before age was I amidst such notions
Yet the pain formed soon into thunderstorm

The faint anguished tears gushes endlessly
Amply deserting my soul lifelessly

-Uzan Swu

I didn't mean to catch your gaze, I simply turned,
and there you were, looking at me, as if fate had
orchestrated our meeting.

-Rukuthonu Vitsu

THE SILENT OBSERVER

In crowded streets where strangers roam,
I am but a silent tome,
Observing minds that ebb and flow,
In the labyrinth where thoughts bestow.

Eyes like windows, bare soul,
In still moments, I stand and gape,
Enchanted by the quite spectacle,
Of dreams and fears that cease and lapse.

In wrinkled brows and passing grins,
In hushed tones and longing miles,
I glimpse the tales left untold,
In silver hearts, hearts of gold.

What vision might dance behind those eyes?
What mysteries in their silent sighs?
I wonder as I stroll by,
In this theatre beneath the sky.

Each face a canvas, each gaze a story,
Of love and loss, of ships set sail,
In the tapestry of human kind,
A cosmos of thoughts I find.

So, I'll remain the silent one,
In the orchestra that's just begun,
watching minds that rise and roam,
In this grand theatre called "Home."

-Rukuthonu Vitsu